WI

Larks!

What Larks!

Poems by Richard Maitland

THE CHOIR PRESS

First published in the United Kingdom in 2015 by
The Choir Press

ISBN 978-1-910864-26-5

Contents

What Larks!   2

Anagramatically Yours   7

Animal Rights   8

A Poet Confesses   10

Are Words Enough?   11

Ars Gratia Artis   12

Autres Temps, Autres Moeurs   13

Bedrock   14

Beginning Again   15

Be Prepared   17

Believing We See   18

Brass Tacks   20

Capturing Life   21

Changes   23

Climate Change   24

Conditions   26

Crossing The Border   28

Cuckoo   29

Days of Glory   30

Dizzyland   32

Drinking Companions   33

Emily   34

Facts are Facts   35

Family Matters   36

Fancy Dancing   37

Feeding The Masses   38

Freedom   39

Freewheeling   41

Gardener's Question Time   42

Goldrush   43

Goodies And Baddies   44

Growing Up   45

Guilty By Association   46

In A Lonely Place   48

Innocence   49

Insurrection   50

It's Different Now   51

Keeping In Touch?   52

Life At School   53

Life Being Life   55

Listen Up   56

Literally?   57

Looking At Life   58

Looking For Answers   59

Metaphorically Speaking   60

Milkbank Quartet   61

Miss Take?   70

More Than Equal   71

Mr Big   72

Nipped In The Bud   73

Only A Labourer   74

On The Level 76

Opportunism   77

Orouborus   78

O.S.S.   79

Other Things Being Equal   80

Paul   81

Playing To Win   82

Polyopathy   84

Polythemous   85

Problem Child   87

Senses Matter   88

Sleepwalking   89

Speaking To Jean   90

Special Favours   92
Strong Men Feed On Iron   93
Suffering Art   94
Suffer The Little Children ...   95
Sunset Street   96
Takeover   98
Terminus   99
The Best-Of-All Tools   100
The Facts Of Life   101
The Man Who Swallowed The World   102
Them And Us   103
Then, And Now   104
Tyger, Tiger   106
Uncertainties   107
Under Cover   108
We All Have Our Moments   109
What Did I Say?   111
Who's Who?   112
Witness   113
Wordsmith   115
Why Ears?   117
Short Poems   119

Dedication

'To my brother Joe, life-long friends Dave and Chris, wife, companion and best pal, Dorothy – for criticism, correction and patience. My eternal thanks.'

What Larks

What Larks!

Visible always, even at dark
Joe Gargery and his: "What Larks!"
A blacksmith, proud of his skill and trade,
complete at birth, and perfectly made.
His 'prentice Pip, by way of chance,
having the choice to gain advance.
But thinking: No, no, no.
I'm happy here, with Joe.
Yet through the night, sleeps not a wink.
And in the morning, comes to the brink;
When Joe says: "Seeing you've had no rest,
old chap, I'll tell you now, adventuring's best.
And you were just the lad.
What larks! What larks to be had."

In London, Pip meets Herbert Pocket;
Acquaintance, mentor, gentleman, friend.
Lodging together is such a pleasure,
they both relax, and overspend.
Parties, dinners, nights out with the 'Finches';
Lessons by Herbert on etiquette,
re-fashion Pip from smith's apprentice
to Gentleman; complete, correct.

But earning and spending are still out of kilter
when Joe, the blacksmith, taps on the door.
Sits at the table, awkward, embarrassed.
Eats with a cough;
drops food on the floor.

Oh Joe, oh Joe. Why did you come?
To escape the countryside's tedium,
that made you so dull and drearisome?
"Begging your pardon, sirs, manners won't do.
I'm much more at home with horses to shoe."
Then go, you fool, and let's forget
that other life, I've learned to regret.
God forbid, it should ever recur;
Pip I was, but have risen to, Sir.
"So hear my news, and that is all:
Estella is home, and wants you to call.
Miss Havisham bidded me come and say
as much; and now I'll be on my way."
Then he was gone, without any "What larks."
and Pip, ashamed of former remarks,
clung to the knowledge, no words had been said:
But remained concealed in his heart and head.
Estella, Estella. Yes, he would go,
and perhaps, have time to visit Joe …
… He stepped from the coach with good intention:
But the sight of Estella was a vote for abstention.
And soon, he would have to go …

… At home in Barnard's Inn, he learned
that Mrs Joe had passed away.
And he must make a quick return
to be at sister's funeral day.

"You might have written," Pip said to Biddy,
"and let me know Mrs Joe was ill."
"Might I, Mr Pip?" repeated Biddy.
"When others have duties, they don't fulfil?"
"But some are busier than others, you know.
I told you before; I intend to see Joe …"
"Intent, you may have, but what wins the prize?
Promises fail, when humours arise."
She couldn't have known those words would be
the hallowed seeds of prophecy.

Too much confusion in head and heart:
distracts attention from other cares,
which first decline, then fall apart;
until at last, the heart despairs.
And now in debt, his patron dead.
Pip, sick with a fever, takes to his bed.
Worries and fears, by sickness portrayed
as bailiffs, demanding debts must be paid.
Struggling to rise, and settle their claims,
faintly a voice all anxiety tames.
"Joe, is it you?"
"Which it air, old chap.
Take it easy, dear Pip. You've had quite a nap.
We'll soon build you up to your old self again
with little, but lots – excluding Champagne!
And walk by the Thames, on countryside trips.
What larks. What larks. Watching seagulls 'n ships!"

And so they did.
Slowly at first, but as Pip improved,
something in their relationship moved
to push them further apart. Was Pip the one to blame?
Of course, he was. Relapsing once more to the same
pompous bore who'd succeeded in little, and ended in
shame.
"You're stronger now, Pip, old chap."
"I couldn't have managed without your care."
"You have your rest, I'll say goodnight:
But whenever you need me, I'll be there."

Next morning though, Joe was gone.
And in his place, a letter,
which read: *Not wishing to intrude.*
I'll leave, now you are feeling better.
Jo.
P.S. Ever the best of friends.

But what's this here? Another sheet?
He opened it out: "Good Lord, a receipt.
The monies owing amount to . . . nil!
And a certain *Joe Gargery* has signed the bill."
A surge of emotion brought tears to Pip's eyes.
Dear Joe. Dear Joe. A child at heart;
but abundantly wise.

Pip vowed to work abroad and earn,
and settle the debt he owed, on return.
But first, a visit to see Joe once more.
He would stay as guest at the 'Blue Boar'.
But news of his troubles had travelled fast,
and the service was worse than he'd known in the past.
No kindly remarks, no courtesy shown;
He regretted he'd come, and sighed, when alone …
… But at least, slept well, and breakfasting done,
went walking in countryside warmed by the sun.
And thought of its loveliness, this offspring of dirt:
Enhancing all life with oases from hurt.

Joe's forge lay ahead, but hearing no clink
of hammer on metal, he started to think
the worst. And saw its door shut tight.
Panicked a little, then saw the house in light.
White curtains fluttered like butterflies
And there, there stood, to his surprise
Biddy and Joe, both arm in arm,
Safe. Both safe from any harm.
They laughed, and cheered, embraced and wept
But went inside as darkness crept
across the sky. Biddy adjourned
and Joe sat smug; until she returned,
carrying a baby wrapped in a rug.
"It's time you learned, old chap," said Joe.
"Not long arrived, he's almost new,
and blessed with a name
the same as you."

Anagramatically Yours

A funeral is real fun
for those who pay attention.
Eleven plus two
is twelve plus one,
a very clever invention.

On a scale of sin
a confessional
is neither dark, nor light;
so find an inn;
discretional:

And

froth the gin for the night.

Animal Rights

'What a find! What a find! Oh boy. Oh boy.'
He'd been searching around for days.
'Everything's perfect, tidy and new.
Florence will be amazed.'
She couldn't speak when she saw it.
Happiness bright in her eyes.
'Oh Bunny, I can't believe it.
This is the highest of highs.
No more looking here and there.
No burrowing through soil and stone.
No furniture to haul around.
At last, a place to call our own.'

. . .

"The Secret Life of Rabbits.
The programme of the Year.
We'll double our rating easily.
And I'll be a millionaire!"
"But boss, its all been done before.
Or have you something up your sleeve?'
'Of course, I have, and it's a wow.
I'll tell you now. It's real. Believe.
An amateur's made a speech-decoder,
that lets us know what animals say.
We've fixed one up for the programme tonight.
Herbert, we're on our way."

. . .

"Good evening ladies, and gentlemen.
Tonight your viewing will be unique.
Tonight you'll witness rabbits talking,
and understand the words they speak.

And here they come to the home we built
with every luxury money could buy ..."
"No sound? No sound? The Anitran's dead?
Forgive me listeners, I'm going to cry.

But wait, something's happening:
They're both knelt down on the floor.
She's got a marker and paper:
Two batteries are in his right paw."

"She's writing. She's writing a message ...
And now, they're holding it high ...
It's wonderful, it's super. It's ...

THANKS FOR OUR HOME, AND –

GOOD-BYE."

A Poet Confesses

Pregnant with poems, I've carried so long
sonnets and ballads, sestinas and songs;
satires, rondels, pastiches and odes;
some of them tigers, some of them toads.
Some half-forgotten as soon as you've read 'em;
Others dismissed, when I stood up and said 'em.
They're the amphibians, if you haven't guessed,
But sharp teeth and claws, are me at my best.
There's nothing like blood and a whole lot of gore
to stir up my passions and make me want more.
The thrill of the chase, the power of hope,
lives in the veins of poets like Pope.
But now, what I see, disappoints and upsets:
People with crocs and hippos as pets.
Magnificent beasts, paraded in mirth
to secure their owners a spoonful of worth.
Give an excuse for conversation:
"The English are such an eccentric Nation ...
and all the way from Bukavu ...
I can't believe it! Can you? Can you?"
Oh yes. I understand too well,
the circus clown, the carousel.
The fiction that we take for real:
This *ersatz* life ...

... distractions can't heal.

Are Words Enough?

Are words enough when courage fails
and would-be heroes turn their tails?
Pro patria mori may sound fine,
after a steak and bottle of wine:
But if fighting a foe of evil design,
self-preservation prevails.

Are words enough when Passion foils
all good intentions, and grabs the spoils.
But sated, the doer denies intent.
Blaming occasional devilment
on poverty, and youth misspent:
From which he now recoils.

The judge has heard it all before.
But lying's not against the Law,
And when the girl involved says, "Yus,
ah led 'im on." It didn't impress.
Defence defeated, had no redress
and the judge began to snore.

Words can bring justice, or bring it to halt.
Some people, as judges, aren't worth their salt.
But let us proceed without further ado,
and decide if our question is false, or true.
Words **are** enough, to give them their due:

It's people themselves,

at fault

Ars Gratia Artis

A potter makes a pot with clay.
Sprinkling water on the way
and shaping it with skill.
A painter first begins to sketch
a blue two-masted, fishing ketch;
Washing it then, until
the paper is smooth and fit
for painting, bit by bit.

Invention and reality
produce the final mix
that radiates from every work
without the use of tricks.

A poet uses words to weave
a tapestry of make-believe,
in colours meant to charm and please
the children, who in former times,
repeated Humpty Dumpty rhymes:
Delightfully, at ease.

Art for Art's sake is no measure:

Children's laughter is twice the treasure.

Autres Temps, Autres Moeurs

Sexual intercourse for me
began in 1973,
when I was nearly thirty.
Some fourteen-year-olds today would sneer,
who'd already started their own career
way back in infant school:
Because they thought it 'cool'.

But even in 1964
at twenty one, I knew no more
than what my mother had told me.
Of course, by then, I'd altered view
on what was false, and what was true
concerning the weaker sex:
Especially, in the Rex.

Before I had the key to the door.
The cinema's dark gave a chance to explore . . .
. . . but still, it never went very far:
Before
Lights on,
and

au revoir.

Bedrock

Talking in bed
to one, long dead,
comforts me now and then.
But when I awake,
the same old ache
tortures my heart again.
Do I awake inside a dream,
that shields me, more than thought?
Or, are convictions I assume,
the very chains that have me caught?

Language and Logic set us apart
to create a world of our own.
But words betray our faith in them;
Philosophers have shown.

If words demean the thing they name,
as Nietzsche boldly asserts.
Familiar and strange
are both within range:

But oh, how the pain of you

hurts.

Beginning Again

Somehow the life I took for real
no longer has the same appeal:
But, stepping back in Time I've found
another life, where joys abound.

Where Angels glory and rejoice
above a shrill, and cackling voice:
To make it sweet, and thus ensure
that Innocence and Faith endure.

Remembering those former times:
The stories, songs and nursery rhymes.
which cherished Hope, and worshipped Chance:
Perfumed the days and praised Romance.

When birds and ants were still prepared
to work and help and show they cared
for people; those in greater need:
Victims of power, envy and greed.

Gathered together, one and all –
as if for a celebratory ball,
– living as Lords with jelly and cake.
All except one: The son of that snake.

He'd hung around and spied awhile,
ein meisterwerk of glibness and guile
'til under his skin he started to itch:
Sloughed it off quickly, revealing a witch.

The witch I mentioned once before:
Who beckoned me in then locked the door.
Until a truth, once held so bright
was vanquished, and replaced by night.

No sedative could give me ease,
when living had become disease.
Until by chance, the Fate's combined
to send an Angel soft and kind:

And bless the tapestries we weave

around our lives

of Make-Believe.

Be Prepared

Ants are Nature's robots.
Bees are much the same.
Pavlovian reactions
hard wired into the brain.
Stimuli evoke response.
Insects have no choice.
Mechanically obeying
their Mother's silent voice.
All are One, but one's not all.
Yet still, he must obey.
And add his might
when there's a fight,
to help secure the day.

Animals have bigger brains
But Instinct's their default.
When danger threatens calf or cub,
neurons come to a halt.
Tooth and claw, ferocious speed:
Surprise the younger male
who's caught off guard, because naïve,
but lives to tell the tale.

Humans have the biggest brain,
but have to pay the cost
of losing ancient abilities
the others never lost.
Detached, distracted, ill at ease,
embracing only what is new.
With no default to save the day:

Nor substitute in lieu.

Believing We See

Seeing myself with other eyes,
there'd be a difference, I surmise.
But exactly what, I couldn't say:
It's hard to be oneself today.

For who we are, we never know.
The fact of facts is the cracks they show.
Outside and inside remain aloof
between the two there's little truth.

Consider the eye's physiology.
It's much the same, for you or me.
(And if it's not, let's just pretend:
Or else, this poem is at an end.)

We see, but do not see at all:
And though her looks may still enthral,
a lady in her loveliness.
is not as we believe, but less.

She's not the photograph, we think:
But product of a different link.
Both eye and brain in combination
form this phantom of creation.

And yet, it's often held as true –
depending on one's point of view –
that seeing is believing:
And not, as Self-deceiving.

Blind spots are never there to see,
but mirages do appear to be.
And optical illusions force
a childish grin, we all endorse.

Sight's not the most reliable tool,
and doesn't always play by rule.
But without it, where would humanity be?

Still stuck right here:

Believing we see.

Brass Tacks

A stereotype does not exist
as does a cat, a bat, or frog.
Instead, it shelters in the brain;
accompanied by surrounding fog.
Much as a sentry standing on guard
or cardboard King on a playing card,
ready for action, without dispute,
although a counterfeit substitute.

But also a joker, who'll laugh, when alone,
at gullible humans, confusing a fake
with the laughing Buddha inside them all;
who taught that they must stay awake.
Stay awake, and be aware
of body, mind and Folly's call.

Stereotypes are Nature's lame ducks.

For nothing's fixed, and all's in a flux.

Capturing Life

When making love to a woman
it's gently, gently, my friend.
Words instead of actions
are what I'd recommend.

Lower your voice a little
and make it deep and slow.
Praising whatever pleases
you, but always adagio.

Pleasure she wants, as much as you
but, not so quickly, not so fast.
Speed is not the issue here:
The winner's the one who comes in last.

And not the hero, muscle-bound
with laughing eyes in sunburnt face,
but he, forgetful of himself,
who's well aware there is no race.

The very opposite of life
around the busy world today,
where Speed and Time are paramount:
But rife in Mandalay.

For Mr Kipling's now the name,
seen in the adverts on T.V.
No longer the bard of the Empire;
forgotten by all but we

poets. The bearers of the flame
that flickers now and then,
when absolutes are trumpeted
in many a lonely glen.

Is this what's known as living?
Forgetting the world of old?
Spending our days of pleasure,
counting our piles of gold?

Always in such a hurry,
even when sitting at home,
with thoughts demanding attention:

A portrait, in monochrome.

—◦◦◦◦—

Changes

He looked at the mirror again;
the twisted filigree
depicting the whole world
in gold. Such luxury
once was his. But now,
exiled from Rome by Augustus,
dependent on his wife's good will,
he cursed them both for their injustice,
setting his worth at nil.

Publius Ovidius Naso,
the toast of literate Rome;
equal of Virgil and Horace,
sat down in a temper, to finish his poem.
A magnum opus, model for all
to read; to celebrate: This, his aim.
And make, at last, a work supreme:
'Metamorphoses' would be its name.
Recounting how the world began;
of man's beginnings, myths and gods;
of heroes and heroines
who'd fought and won, against all odds.

Foretelling the future of Rome: yet annoyed
by a mirror …
reflecting

what's void.

Climate Change

Everything changes, Heraclitus said
a long time ago, or thereabouts.
Now, today, they're saying the same:
Though I for one, have got my doubts.

For what precisely are the grounds,
when common sense is out of bounds?
And all the facts presented us
are limited by radius.

To understand an entity
(because that's what the Earth must be)
it's not enough to take a figure
by itself. We must think bigger.

For when the figure meets its ground:
The two together will abound
in other facts, unseen before:
That leave us trembling, filled with awe.

There's Earth in Time, and Earth in Space.
The Earth we know as commonplace.
The Earth inside, that groans and spews
her insides out, and fills the News.

There's Earth as friend, and Earth as foe
as species come, and species go.
So listen up, you simian freaks:
We're just another bunch of geeks

who pride ourselves on being smart:
Forgetting we must soon depart,
just like the others, long since gone,
whose time was up, as Number One.

But still we spin our webs of thought
to catch a Truth, that we abort,
when brighter brains as yet, unknown:
Devise a theory all of their own . . .

Meanwhile the Earth is past concern:
Sometimes she'll freeze, sometimes she'll burn.

Whatever happens, it's nothing new.

As Heraclitus, that old Greek knew.

Conditions

Hating the man I'd called my friend
these poisonous lines to him are penned:

You, sir, afford me no delight.
You're ugly, fat and just the sight
of you shambling, ambling, in the street
provokes a very quick retreat.

I will not face you, sir, again
unless it be to wish you pain.
And plant a notion in your mind
so all your thoughts, you'll never find,

as they go whizzing round your head
so fast, that nothing can be said
for days and weeks and maybe years
until that notion disappears.

Or I might choose another path
to make you laugh and laugh and laugh
though nothing's funny, not one bit
and others, think you've lost your wit.

For I'm a wizard who has the power
to tame the wind or change the hour.
Bring on the rain, or stir the sun
from sleepiness: And when I've won

turn all that's dark back into day
after telling stars that they can stay
still visible and shining bright
as they did before, when it was night.

And havoc will annihilate
that treacherous friend I've come to hate.
For I'm the author of this text
and his betrayal has me vexed.

As twins we were, and still could be
if he'd respect authority,
I'd welcome him back into the Club:

My dear old friend,

Beelzebub.

Crossing The Border

MacDonald Fraser wrote a book,
Sir Walter Scott another.
The first took care that facts were right;
the other didn't bother.
An Army service fathered one,
the other, Imagination sired.
But both when published, selling well,
were very much admired.
Sir Walter won the hearts of boys
by action, bravery, and guile.
MacDonald Fraser told his tale
in disciplined prose of sober style.

But each had crossed the Border lands
before the rule of King and Law,
and rode with Reivers of both sides:
Adventures they couldn't ignore,
on Galloway ponies, deep-chested, keen,
whatever the weather, or terrain,
to get in the lead and hold off the rest;
whatever discomfort, whatever the pain.
Their riders too, blood on the rise,
readied their lances, checked their dirks …
All correct, and battle joined;
though no-one's hurt:

And absence,
irks.

Cuckoo

In lines across the page,
a poem of mine is printed.
Words humanised in style,
but deviously minted.
Words with the weight of solid coins
of differing shapes and sizes.
But, in addition, as living things:
Brimming with Life's surprises.
Foremost, their identity:
Never take it for granted.
They look content,
but still ferment,
by Lucifer, enchanted.

A child may answer to a name
long held in great renown.
But later on, that paragon
will opt for: William Brown.
Approach each stranger with some care.
A hand outstretched, may move to slap.
Be hesitant, and don't commit:
For Yes or No, could be a trap.

And take your time. It's hard to beg.
For poems are more like cuckoo's eggs:
Accepted only in snatches.
And must be sat on, now and then:

Before the durn thing hatches.

Days Of Glory

When I was young
and Angels sung
to celebrate each day:
Then coaxed the Sun
on his daily run,
I shouted hip hooray.

And skipped and ran
to join my clan –
the other girls and boys
who'd pleaded and cried
to be outside
and join in making noise.

Yelling and shouting,
chasing around.
Hiding away
where they'd always be found.

Jumping and hopping
and kicking a ball
Biting their tongue
when it came to a fall.

Then up again quickly
and still in control,
dribbling like Matthews ...
and scoring a goal.

When I was young
and Angels sung
I lived each day to the full.
But now I'm old
and life's on hold,
the prospect's dark and dull.

And yet, inside
myself, a tide
brings thoughts to which I cling.
And then, and then
I hear again
those golden Angels sing.

ॐ

Dizzyland

Reality is fantasy
for many modern folk.
Infantilised, and patronized
by those who get the joke.
Bread and circuses win again,
as once they did before.
When Romans ruled over much of the world
in those good old days of yore.

But now, we're all electrified.
Citizens of the Web.
With access to a Universe
I hope will never ebb.
Cyber Citizens safe at home;
venturing anywhere.
Safari parks in Africa,
Climbing the Alps, without a care.
The latest app has multi functions,
built from experiences caught complete,
from volunteers in hundreds of thousands:
So everyone able can now repeat.

. . .

My dad said, son. Don't be a dreamer.
Work hard. Be honest. Drink only tea.
But I became a Pluto-crat:
And now, the world belongs
to
ME.

Drinking Companions

I wrote a poem that wriggled like a fish;
and couldn't reel him in, without a fight.
It happened one fine summer's day,
but ended when the moon was shining brightly.

Unhooking him, I gathered up my kit.
He flip-flopped on the sandy beach awhile.
But when, at last, my gear was packed away,
I walked across the sand to see him smiling.

"Begorrah, but you're quite the man, you are.
I've never met the likes of you before.
Hercules himself, you'd put to shame.
I cannae go, without I know your name."

I'd had a dram or two, I must confess.
But a Highland single malt fills me with zest.
It stimulates the brain, and warms the heart:
A brew no other brew could be contesting.
"The name is Mungo," I answered him then;
and poured a wee dram to celebrate.
He sniffed and drank, like a connoisseur ...

And thanked me again at breakfast:
Smiling upwards

from my plate.

Emily

"Is the sky a cover, or carpet?"
Emily asked her mum.
"Don't ask such silly questions,
remember, school's to come.
We've only got ten minutes,
and have to pick up your chum.

Emily left the kitchen,
and heard dad flushing the loo.
"Is the sky a cover, or carpet?"
"I haven't the slightest clue.
But Granddad knows, if anyone does:
He was one of The Few."

Emily found her Granddad,
and tried her question once more.
Repeated it a second time,
And then he said: "The war?
We won, you know. But long ago:
And I've forgotten the score."

So Emily ran to the garden,
and looking straight up at the sky.
Pleaded with God for an answer:

But never received a reply.

Facts Are Facts

Is this a documentary?
This programme on the BBC.
Being shown by Mrs Ritter,
that's causing her infants to squirm and titter?
Says one: "It's only a three-act play,
with little factual on display;
And for this my dad pays a licence?"
The others clap their hands in glee,
"I'm sick of mediocrity,"
says Mary Jane Monroe.
"Act One is always such a bore.
We've seen it so many times before.
The Setup, as they call it."
"And then the villain comes along,"
to make the hero's day go wrong,"
adds Billy Green, complaining.
"Now children, don't let's get excited.
There's many a wrong that needs to be righted;
but listen to what I say.
Throughout the war, the BBC
gave Europe hope and guarantee
of Liberty, Truth and Victory.
The Nazi hordes had conquered all,
except for Britain – still standing tall.
Completely undefeated ..."
Billy Green put up his hand.
"Thank you, Miss. We understand.
Facts are facts, not fiction:

It's their absence, that's causing this friction."

Family Matters

Gold was for treacle, and green for us.
Children of war who were taught not to fuss
at minor abrasions, or the sight of our blood;
but use fingers as plasters wherever we could.
I'd learned it all from my soldier-dad,
who neutralised tears by saying: "My lad . . ."
and telling a tale he said he'd heard
of a man whose head was chopped off by a sword:
Yet **he'd** never said a word.

Now it was treacle, way out in space,
with no-one about to give us a chase.
Golden syrup from Tate and Lyle;
whose discarded tins gave reason to smile.
That was our mission, and when it was done
my chosen crew were ready for fun.
Explorers all, adventure-fond,
we'd reached our goal, but now looked beyond;

and found the Aliens in a pond.
Not cowering, but unaware.
that we, their enemies, were standing there.
I pocketed one, to show as a prize:

But dad just looked, and to my surprise,
said: "Take him home, son . . .

. . . to his kiddies, and wives."

Fancy Dancing

Reality takes some believing
by those of us bent on achieving
other-acting ways.
Let me explain our constant doubt,
in living a life that's inside out;
dispersing mental haze.

Today is built upon the Past,
but Tomorrow's racing bullet-fast,
to push her back into line.
While others fall like dominoes
devoid of life, and other woes,
who once, were leonine.

But still, they're with us – all the way;
those artificers of Yesterday.
Once the bad boys of the block
whose poetry was poppycock –
or so, the critics complained,
when other values obtained.

Today the aye's combine with no's.
Imagination swops its clothes,
at leisure, when it will.
And what is reel, but make a show,
in audio, or video:

And dance a fancy quadrille?

Feeding The Masses

A hundred thousand babies
spawned by a single mum,
who cuddles and caresses them,
until their time has come.
A hundred thousand babies
who very often feud
when, once released, and on their own
compete in the race for food.
Fighting for every morsel;
using both strength and speed,
when joined by brothers and sisters
having the self-same need.

Mother looks, and worries –
if only life were fair,
but well she knows, it isn't;
and one must not despair.
Enough of them will manage
to pass the tests ahead.
And with her help, if need be,
they'll live, when she is dead.

Aware that the weather is changing,
this octopus never stops trying,
but offers herself as the protein they need:
and keeps them alive, by

dying.

Freedom

I am a bird
a little bird
who's heard
the call of Spring
and feels the urge
to mix and merge
with others on the wing.

but I'm the pet
of an ageing vet,
my saviour, and sage,
who asks me why
I want to fly
when I've
a nice warm cage.

'Outside
Outside
both wind and tide
will blur the brightest vision
and rain and storm
will soon reform
a juvenile decision.

Stay put. Stay put.
And I'll not shut
the door of your cage
again.
and you'll be free
the same as me
to live without the pain.'

The offer, tough.
The smooth or rough?
Should I stay, or go?
The cowardly me
said: 'I agree.'
But a voice inside said: 'No.'

So I said, 'Yes'
and as you've guessed
that was vital key.
An open door
I couldn't ignore:

Freedom had set me free.

Freewheeling

Reality is Gravity
wearing another face.
Set in a frown
to keep life down;
Far away from that happier place.
No, I don't mean Heaven.
I'm not a believer as such.
But would rather remain
in touch with the brain
to use a more physical crutch ...
Though, even so,
It's to and fro
whether or not, that's true.
We all have a skull,
the Bright and the Dull;
But brains are physical too.
Where am I going?
What will I find?
By dropping the brain,
in favour of Mind?
(Maybe that's being unkind.)
Yet Mind's the seat of consciousness;
of thought, volition and feeling.
And that's the place I love to be.
The site I'm now revealing:

Where Fantasy's freewheeling.

Gardeners' Question Time

Is life another fiction?
Reality a con?
Belief, a contradiction
no sooner here, than gone?

Is love the mind's delusion,
when hormones start to soar?
A chemical confusion,
that shakes us to the core.

Unsettles our insanity
with urges thoroughly sane.
Pooh-poohing mankind's vanity:
With visceral disdain.

Is death an end to living?
No matter how defined.
Or God's ironic giving
of gifts to which we're blind?

'What is truth?' said Jesting Pilate,
quickly leaving the scene.
Was he a shrinking violet?

Or merely an aubergine?

Goldrush

Remembering is not for me.
The Past's a room without a key,
in which to dump old memories,
and watch them slowly rotting.
Memories both good and bad,
that tempted me when still a lad.
Until I learned that absentees
are very soon forgotten.
And lived my life as one long day.
Accepting praise that came my way,
from parents proud to see a boy:
And thinking, they were winning.
So I was worshipped from above
by smiling faces bright with love,
who gave food and kept me warm:
A promising beginning.
But childhood passes, and soon I learned
such adulation must be earned,
by working hard, deep underground,
in constant heat and toil.

Chapel on Sundays: Praise the Lord.
Comforted by the Holy Word
that follows faithfully, homeward bound:

No Greed or Wickedness can soil.

Goodies And Baddies

To be good is to please the others;
our mother and father, sisters and brothers.
Teachers and classmates, the parents of friends.
Not falling out, but making amends.
Laughing and singing, or skipping with rope,
not sitting at home, unable to cope
with cutting remarks about our behaviour;
but ignoring the slight, as they do in Belgravia.

To be good is not to ask questions,
or make academic suggestions
which bamboozle all other folk;
Who'll never believe, it's a joke.
And even if laughter's hard won,
never correct any slip of the tongue:
It's a sin only fools recommend,
and will do us no good in the end.

To be bad is harming or hurting.
Breaking the rules, or reverting
to force. In order to get our own way,
by putting our faults on display.
To be bad makes us all, sick with sin.
Witnessing pain with a grin
and cussing and cursing,
instead of conversing
as Ladies, now and then:

Civilly, like Gentlemen.

Growing Up

Reality's been slapping me
around for years and years.
While others seem to carry on
as if they had no cares.
Money's no problem. Relationships, fine.
Always at parties, swimming in wine.
Not that I am envious, only to relate
how differences matter, when tempered by Fate.

Extroverts and introverts are those I have in mind
that like so many other words,
have changed, and been re-defined.
Extroverts were gregarious, and Introverts were shy.
Now it's about the stimuli, boosting them both up high.
The first needs other people to make their engines spark.
The second is self-promoting, and works alone, in the dark.
But once, these names were absolute, you either were, or not.
Now you could be, more or less, and who knows what is what?

Myself, I've given up the Quest,
because I'm fully grown.
Understanding what Garbo meant:
In pleading for life

alone.

Guilty By Association

'I hope you're feeling well today',
Robby said, greeting me.
'Would you like a rum and coke,
or nice, sweet cup of tea?'
Of course, he didn't speak like us,
but I could read his eyes.
Contracting and dilating –
changing colour and size.

I'd lived in the Martian colony
ten years before the war.
Learning their language as a child:
When Home wasn't Home any more.
But now the Four have mounted their steeds,
Travelling far and wide.
Bringing disease, famine and Death
to Cities and countryside.

For flesh is soft, and soon gives way
whenever attacked full force.
From inside or outside, by germ or shell.
And even, Trojan horse.
A remnant survived and fled their Mother:
To Mars and its colony.
People and Robots working together,
thanks to the power of 'D'.

The 'D' control devised by chance
before the Robots' assault.
Allowing us here to curb it's spread,
and bring our fears to a halt.
A simple device that warned in advance,
and stopped interference inside
system control by computers on Earth:
Without which, we, too, would have died.

Without emotions, Robots are slaves.
They have no sense of being.
Requests are orders they'll obey,
never disagreeing.
But trojanized, they'll cease all kneeling,
so overwhelmed by thought and feeling.
And living now, not dead,
will show their faces red.

To test a Robot under suspicion,
use a simple word like 'Hate'.
I say it, and complete my mission.

Robby shows red:

But moves, too late.

In A Lonely Place

"Sure I killed her. I've killed others too."
The detective smiled. "Okay, I've seen
your movies, and know how you feel.
But you're a suspect. It's only routine."
"She came around to read a script,
then took a taxi back to town."
"Anyone see you, after she'd left?"
"A stunning blonde in a dressing gown."
The copper nearly swallowed his gum.
"She lives over there, and please, don't succumb."

But when alone, regretting his cracks,
Dix pictured her dead, cold and still.
And cursed the devils who urged him on;
against a weak, and weary Will.
The doorbell rang, and pulled him back
from black despair. It took a while.
"It's me again. Police? All clear."
And cheered his heart with a genuine smile.
"Come in. Come in. Coffee or tea?"
"They say tea comforts; that's for me."

Their future together couldn't be brighter:
Except for the devils hidden inside.
United now in murderous passion,
to groom the groom,

and exclude the Bride.

Innocence

Do dreams come true?
They did, when you
agreed to share my bed.
For being young and healthy,
I knew, what wasn't said.
At school that's all we talked about,
when free to have our say.
Out in the yard, gathered in groups,
pretending to be at play.

The Masters knew. Of course, they must.
As men, they too felt carnal lust.
Suffering fantasy's fatal lure;
For which, thank God, He made no cure;
but promised only as time went by,
that we would flourish and multiply.

And set no proper time to start.
That's why; at last, I'm taking part.
And all ablaze with hormonal yen;

Except, except.
You didn't say:

When.

Insurrection

Another night without a poem
to add to my collection;
It would have been one hundred and four
without this insurrection.
Rebellion of a feminine sort,
by her who may be having sport,
considering my rejection.
Call it ego if it fits
or something worse, that Law permits.
My conscience won't be scarred.
I did the only thing I could:
As any other artist would,
who found himself debarred.

What's life, beside a work of art?
A slovenly, unloved old tart
Jack would cut up with glee.
I asked politely, if she'd oblige,
but over the phone, heard only sighs.
No hint of *bonhomie*.
Burning inside with surging ire,
I piled my poems upon the fire.

Watched them blacken and start to burn:
All for a Muse,
who's taciturn.

It's Different Now

It doesn't have to rhyme to be a poem.
The Muses are three gals who like to roam.
Old Rockers would describe them all as 'ravers'
who, passing on, might well bestow their favours
on anyone, who may not be ideal,
but has that helpless, animal appeal.

It doesn't have to rhyme to be a poem.
A painter isn't tied to monochrome;
or forced to work with canvas, using brushes
to capture his model's scarlet-coloured blushes.
No, no. He needs some freedom to express
meanings so esoteric, we're left to guess.

Sculptors as well, use abstract forms to tease us.
Owing to Rodin's attempts to pleasure, and please us.
Producing figures, critics thought unique:
Naturalistic, but with a modern tweak.
Fragments without an arm, a leg, a head,
as Modern Art, in fashion, quickly spread.
And this is how it is, even today,
though some may find it boring or blasé.
I trust that you'll enjoy my paradigm –

And understand, why poems

don't need to rhyme.

Keeping In Touch?

What an achievement, three billion miles!
Scientists' faces all wreathed in smiles.
It's taken nine years, but no fits or starts
clouded the joy of adventurous hearts.
New Horizon, nothing adverse,
a tiny speck in the universe,
but nuclear powered and crowded with gear;
on course to Pluto, and now very near.
Sensors measuring winds from the Sun
Imagers capturing pictures that stun
NASA controllers astonished, remark:
"Now at last, we can see in the dark."
For Pluto is mostly cloaked in night.
Far from the Sun and its warmth and light.

But now, by means of substitution,
we humans need no absolution
to trespass in God's abode.
(Technology's got Him buffaloed.)

Controllers at NASA hoot and holler,
though no-one imagines, what must follow.
To all unbelievers, God makes riposte.

As screens go blank,

and contact is lost.

Life At School

Home from school at eight years old
to find my entrance blocked:
And try the handle once again,
but the door's securely locked.

Twice this week. Where is she now?
I kick the door in vain.
Does she really care for me?
Leaving me here in the rain.

That's when I thought, I'll build a hut,
beside the next door shed.
A shelter of my very own,
with comics and books, instead

of waiting. Waiting. Waiting. Not
knowing how long she'll be.
Making me feel unwanted:
Making a fool of me.

With all my heart, I loved her once.
Since then, I've learned to doubt.
She's not the girl she used to be
when ever I'm about.

It's just as if she's someone else,
and living under a spell.
She hardly smiles or speaks to me:
Perhaps she's just unwell.

I asked my dad, if it was true:
He looked at me in surprise.
"From the mouths of babes", he said at last,
with teardrops misting his eyes.

No sign of Mother at breakfast next day.
Father sat solemn and stern.
"Ready for school?" he said, when we'd done:

"Children have lots to learn."

—⊶◉◉⊷—

Life Being Life

In fairy tales, and Disney films
the Damsel's good, the Dragon's a cad.
For adults know, a child must learn
the difference 'twixt Good and Bad.
Churches and schools together act
to reinforce what's writ in stone.
No-one asks what goodness means
in situations still unknown.
Ordinary happenings in streets, or towns
that other citizens wisely ignore.
Knowing too well, the life that's theirs
has good and bad at an open door:
That One can change; become the Other;
caught in a strange revolving game
propelled by sudden emotional surges,
because they're fashioned much the same.
Romance, of course, delights in words
that capture the awe of Nature's rages.
Extolling the perfect Beauty there:
Then locks it up on printed pages.

Always the dreamer, my dreams came true
the night we met, and joined as one.
I thought, 'At last. At last I've won.'

But Life being Life,
was soon . . .

. . . undone.

Listen Up

Other poets,
the same as me
have sung of Death
and Uncertainty.
But offered no solutions.

Instead they dither,
and make us wait,
like that Roman Governor,
always late:
Dallying at his ablutions.

When what we want
are words in action;
not another staged distraction
that leaves an unhealthy pong.

But something to treasure,
that's worth the keeping;
even if Life has
left us weeping ...

We'll thankfully go along:

when moved,

by a soothing song.

Literally?

Well, you asked for it. Here it is;
a tumbled up, jumbled up, wordy piece
that's genuine, not jerry-built.
Another windmill at which to tilt;
to fill another day.

The second name of Word is Legion,
especially in the sunlit region
where children are wont to play.
On fields alive with other creatures
butterflies, ladybirds, beetles and such
foreign, and sometimes, funny to touch;
but stimulating conversation
and juvenile imagination:
While using the family crutch

of other words, that have no cargoes
except themselves, estranged from argots,
as universal codes.
Names that Time corrodes,
but still are useful, feeding senses.
Providing life by building fences

around imaginary gardens –

alive with natterjack toads.

Looking At Life

If now I bind myself to verse
it's not for fame, or gain of purse.
But put those notions into reverse,
and you will have a clue.

Interest rates were much too low
for any savings of mine to grow,
and taking a lead from Edgar Poe,
I made a late debut.

It triggered fancies in my brain,
that set at nought financial gain,
and made me as a child again
with pleasures old and new.

Greeting the world with boyhood's wonder
Ripping the cage of words asunder:
Seeing language as Nature's blunder,
and anything, but true.

. . .

"Work hard at school until the bell,"
said mum. "We know that you'll do well.
Richer even that tunc-kan-tel" . . .

and left me to chew it over.

Looking For Answers

Mirrors never show us as we are.
Our left side's right, and right is on par.
The image, seen by us, keeps all that's there;
we're different, and the same; yet unaware.
A statement you might find a tad extreme,
Somewhat like Poe's, 'a dream within a dream.'

And then, of course, there's Dickens' master stooge,
known to all as Ebenezer Scrooge;
who argued against believing in the senses
disordered by the body's own defences,
with Marley's ghost, the source of all unease,
merely a blot of mustard, crumb of cheese.

Since then, the realm of Science has expanded
and such opinions, quickly countermanded,
are back within the fold, as Dr Spence
of Oxford, has shown by common-sense
research; confirming ears can boost our taste;
and prove the senses, multi-faced.

"I think, therefore I am." Descartes said long ago.
But who he was, and what, he didn't know.
Yet Newton's maths stayed solid as rocks
and his Universe worked like the insides of clocks;
till Einstein wound it down by offering the Small:

And now, quantum physics is biggest of All.

Metaphorically Speaking

Up is good, and down is bad.
Feeling blue, is feeling sad.
Black is bad, but good is white.
Darkness a cover, we call the night.

Life is a fluid, empty or full.
People, machines, incredibly dull.
Time is a healer – what a relief!
But can be a stealer, aka a thief.

Understanding is seeing
as knowing, is too.
Birth is arrival, for me and for you.
Essence is central, it equals the heart;
though Importance itself still plays quite a part.

People are plants. Starting low, growing high.

And Time is the Reaper,

who watches them die.

Milkbank Quartet

Retribution

Walking along the Annandale Way,
the old rusted railings tell us a tale:
of hubris or greed, folly or passion,
of man's bellicosity, woman's travail.
Attaining a goal, maintaining it whole.
What more could one want or need?
Attack or defend and stand at the end:
One of the Border breed.

"Romantic rubbish," my wife declared.
"Taxes, finance, or social change."
And once, they paid no tax at all.
Government stopped at the moated grange."
A teacher, retired, but still retaining
knowledge absorbed from an Honours degree.
"Left-wing propaganda," I teased.
"From a Marxist University."

"Fascist," she said. But only in fun,
and then returned to the walk we'd begun.
I soon caught up, and linked her hand:
Sealing a friendship where rain clouds were banned.

"Is that a house? There, in the trees?"
I followed her finger, "Hard to say.
But it's some kind of building, I think I can see …
… No, too many branches in the way."
But Margaret wasn't there.
I looked around. Then heard a cry:
"Donald. Come here! Come here!
But why?
Why?
Why?"

…

Milkbank House a shattered ruin.
Roof caved in, windows all gone.
Geometrically past the pale.
With visitors, any gardener would shun.
Thistles, brambles, bindweed, nettles,
abandoning soil now retrograde.
Easily conquering *Lebensraum*:

Mother Nature's *Stoss-brigade*.

The Man And His Work

A Lowland Scot in Canada.
An entrepreneur who had a goal:
To harness Nature's profligate ways,
and bring them under his own control.
The money needed he already had
from banker friends of similar ilk.
Southern men the same as he,
born beside the Water of Milk.

But now he'd bought the cannery
he pondered on the racial mix.
Immigrants all, including Scots:
The very ones he'd have to fix.
Good workers, yes, whose speech was clear
but still, could be a pain.
Divide and rule was just the tool:
By paying them more, business would gain.

The others of course, didn't matter much:
And quickly learned that he was Boss.
Contented in mechanical jobs,
increasing his profits, while making a loss.
He worked them hard and pared their wages.
A businessman must reach his goal:
And soothe disputes by friendly persuasion,
while keeping his work-force under control.

...

The sockeye salmon weren't aware
of any change, when caught and killed.
Millions survived and spawned, and died,
and Nature's demands were still fulfilled.
Wages improved and people fed.
A wealthy Boss banked more and more:
And later donated considerable sums
to help the Allies win the war.

Peace brought medals and tracts of land.
Titles and honours for hounding the Hun.
Bestowed by His Majesty, George the Fifth,

and yes,

including a Barony won.

The House

When Euclid invented geometry
his mother began to whine.
"My son, my son, what have you done?
What good is this straight line?"
"It's the shortest distance between two points."
" And what two points are they?"
"Any chosen as you like
that lie a length away."
"But how can it go through tree or rock?
Through mountain, forest or hill?"
Euclid smiled, and took her hand.
"Mother, it can't: but will …"

The site had always attracted him
when hunting rabbits, or fishing trout.
And now it all belonged to him:
As deeds in his bank proved beyond doubt.
He stood on the hill by the Water of Milk,
as he'd stood many years before.
But now as the owner: now as the Laird,
still true to the oath he swore.
And watched that tangled plot of land
being tamed by iron teeth;
ancient trees and jutting rocks
and ravelled roots beneath.

"Scottish Baronial? Yes, good choice,"
the architect had said.
And now it stood, defiantly,
on land secured from the dead.
The Laird, delighted, beamed at his wife:
Weakened from bearing their only child.
But willing herself to reciprocate,
as radiantly, she smiled.
"Oh yes, it is magnificent.
A castle fit for a King.
Those turreted towers and battlements:
A treasure to which we'll cling."

But who was he, this man of worth,
determined to succeed?
Who else but one of Britannia's four:

One of the Bulldog breed.

Hostages To Fortune

"Sic transit gloria mundi."
A Roman slave would repeat and repeat
into the ear of the victor:
Reminding him life was bitter-sweet.
But Mother Nature has no slave
to warn her; Still an ancient urge,
possessed by all, can alter fate:
When male and female meet and merge.

He met her as she left the rink,
having admired her form and style.
Blue eyes, red lips and golden hair:
had defeated resistance, and fostered a smile.
Marriage of course, had been a must
but business came first, as well he knew.
Now comfortable, he'd settled his debts,
but never forgot his Scottish feu.

...

Good news! Good news! At last, a son.
A sturdy, well-built, healthy boy.
He held his breath and stayed composed.
Unaware it was Nature's ploy.
Belle looked tired. The doctor's nod
meant: All is well, no need to stay.
Retiring at once, and private now,
he sat and smoked his pipe of clay.

He wasn't one, but half and half:
Neither a Jekyll, nor Mr Hyde.
Neither a Saint, nor steeped in sin,
but a suffering pedant inside.
More sons. More sons, as years went on
and every one was straight and true.
Except the first of his sturdy brood:
Too much like him to be subdued.

A Scotsman still in heart and soul,
the Laird in anger scorned his creed.
Denied his first-born's right to rule.
Then changed his will with furious speed.
Family finished. Split in two.
He never felt pain, despite the loss.
And paid no heed to the chosen son
who, after all, was a surrogate boss.

But late at night, he often heard
the sound of Nature's defiant cry.
Echoing slaves who used to call:

"We who are about to die"…

Miss Take?

Migration isn't something new.
Or where would Scotland be,
if after the Ice Age, years ago,
no-one had bothered to cross the sea?
For everyone comes from somewhere,
whether as foe, or friend.
The Wandering Jew, is me and you –
no matter what we pretend.

From the time of leaving Africa,
men made the world their own.
Slaughtering other forms of life,
so they could rule alone.
And having gained that victory
and conquered continents by stealth.
They then attacked their neighbour's lands,
stealing both cattle, and wealth.

Emboldened now, they made their mark
by axe and plough, and hooves of horse;
with weeping women by their side,
cursing their use of force.
But force it was that won the prize;
though critics since, have said they blamed
the warriors themselves, who'd tamed the world,
and then, assumed,
their chattels:

'Tamed'.

More Than Equal

What does it mean to be alive?
(All other things being equal.)
By which I mean
the same old routine,
of completing steps in sequel.
At least, since Newton figured the laws
that gave Man power, and cut the odds
of solving mysteries, held in awe
by those believing in ancient gods.
But gods can change their shape and form:
And even alter sizes.
Chameleons then,
have nothing on them
when it comes to slick disguises.
Reason and Science led the way
Industry following suite.
And somewhere between
A clockwork machine:
Governed, as if absolute.

So what does it mean to be alive?
If not, disrupting the sequel?
We're part machines
who need routines,
But consider ourselves:

More than equal.

Mr Big

Everyone's equal in the dark
of cinematic bliss.
Becoming someone you are not:
What greater joy than this?
Far better than a witch's spell,
or a druggie's bodily hell.
Not what you are from day to day –
however you are made
by poverty, or mental scars.
There's still that Big Parade,
for you to join up there onscreen:
And dream of, in between.
I used to be an ardent fan,
living inside my head;
while working on the railways,
to get some dough for bread.
Until a movie gave me a clue
to the ways and means of making a coup.

Joining the rackets before Prohibition,
I leapfrogged the ladder by ardent ambition.
Bought politicians and blackmailed the Law,
who'd never seen no-one as ruthless before.
Moved to the movies to gather in all ...
But by then, they were talkies:

And the pictures got small.

Nipped In The Bud

"Is the sky a cover, or carpet?"
Emily asked her mum.
"Don't ask such silly questions,
remember school's to come.
We've only got ten minutes,
and have to pick up your chum."

Emily left the kitchen,
and heard dad flushing the loo.
"Is the sky a cover, or carpet?"
"I haven't the slightest clue.
But Granddad knows if anyone does:
He was one of The Few."

Emily found her Granddad,
and tried the question once more.
Repeated it a second time,
And then he said: "The war?
We won, you know. But long ago:
And I've forgotten the score …"

So Emily, now in the garden,
then made up her mind;
and never said another word,
of an intellectual kind.

Only A Labourer

My father always soothed my pain
by stimulation of the brain,
and telling tales that made no sense
to me, in Childhood's Innocence.
But still, it worked. And very well;
No bleeding leg would make me yell.
Sometimes it hurt, I can't deny,
though no-one ever saw me cry.

And he was pleased, and told me more
of army life in Singapore;
of camels racing near the Nile,
and wrestling monster crocodiles.
His wit was quick, his maths the best:
Always ready with table tests,
And so, increasing my worth at school;
where I no longer played the fool.

At home as well, and man to man;
at cards and dominoes, I began
to challenge him for pride of place;
trumping his King, with an eager Ace.
But knew he wasn't the least bit awed,
when he produced a cribbage board.
"Five cards are dealt, two put away
to make the 'crib' for later play.
The pack is cut, the top card turned,
and play begins: All bridges burned."

In cribbage two-hander, this is the aim;
to beat one's opponent, and win the game.
Matches in holes must keep the count
as points are scored, and tensions mount . . .

Dad was a labourer, eas'ly dismissed.

But also,

a child Psychologist.

On The Level

Darwinism had a kink,
opponents called the Missing Link.

Until, in the 'Fifties, one was found
in Leicestershire's unhallowed ground.

And after a hundred years of doubt,
the platypus was IN, not OUT.

Instead of crying, it's a fake,
the public now, had another take.

Opinions change as years go by,
millions are born,
and millions die.

So if you're unhappy,
all too soon to be 'Gone' ...
think:

Babies are smiling,

and LIFE,

carries on.

Opportunism

The gorgeous nonsense Plato wrote
has had our culture by the throat
for many and many a year.
One charioteer and horses, two
winging across a sky of blue:
Effortlessly, through the air.

But one is noble, the other not.
She's somehow stained with an ugly blot
that cause her feathers to moult.
Contaminated since her birth
Eventually she'll fall to earth:
Finishing with a jolt.

Coleridge was right, of course.
Why blame our sins on one poor horse?
It simply isn't cricket.
And yet the Church, grasping at straws,
Welcomed this tale with several encores:

And so, created the 'Wicked'.

Orouborus

It's been around for many years,
and long may it prevail
against the fashions now in vogue:
And carry on eating its tail.
What better symbol could there be
to put against *The Fall*,
than this concise, and circular form
assuring us, One is All?

But no, our lines are always straight
between beginning and end;
for going around in circles won't pay
wage or dividend.
In doing so, we'd only lose
the comforts we adore,
so much a part of who we are
and want to be, evermore.
But a linear life has one big fault;
turnoffs, there are none.
We come to a stop, and wonder, what next?
Quite unaware, we've gone.

Eight is a figure of different form,
a circular Holy Grail,
in that it ends, where it began:

Like the snake that devours its tail.

O. S. S.

Life is a verb,
and all about doing.
Dying today.
Tomorrow: Renewing.

We may be disguised
in a different shape:
As insect or worm,
instead of an ape.

We may not remember
the glory and joy
of living life
as a girl, or boy.

But one thing remains,
after paying Death's toll:
The only exception:

Our Sovereign Soul.

Other Things Being Equal

Other things being equal,
Beauty's above the rest.
Capturing men's attention,
though not necessarily, best.
I mention, only in passing,
the surface skin, and core.
The first reflecting the other:
Does that apply any more?
For life in consumer society
is focused on what we see.
Designing minds, behind the scenes,
enthralling you and me.

Afterwards, we may wonder,
while driving home from the mall,
just who is doing the driving,
and what is the point of it all?
On the back seat a new television,
'Reduced' at a sale that's for 'Real'.
Though at home, it's one more among others:
Yet no-one questions, the 'deal'.

Whether beautiful, plain, or ugly;
intelligent, or a clot.
And others things being equal:
Tied in a Gordian

Knot.

Paul

Laughter found its home in Paul:
Hearty, handsome, friend to all.
Never serious, never dull.
Living life to the very full.

Built like a boxer,
but more of a child
whose radiance shone
when he laughed; when he smiled.

A father important to those he held dear,
who knew Dad's advice was always sincere.
Abigail, Billy now weeping with mum,
uncertain and anxious of what is to come.

But life carries on, and miseries fade:
Stay with the good times, don't be afraid.
Whatever should happen, you'll weather the squall.

Remembering days being happy, with Paul.

Playing To Win

Cryptic crossword time again.
Facing another defeat.
Dorothy's an all-time champion,
but I've been known to cheat.

Reading the clues out one by one
means I can be a chancer.
Especially when I don't always say
the letters of words in the answer.

Yes, she's the girl I chose for my wife
as sweet as sugarcane.
But soon found out, to my surprise,
this baby had a brain.

And now we've both got equal scores,
two questions more to go.
But wait, I've found a three-letter word:
Hooray and tally-ho!

'Ten down', I say, and read the clue
'Strange duck, Donald Duck'.
(But that's a cod.)
"*And how many letters?*"
'I'm sorry, three ...
... and the answer is 'odd'.

I say it quickly to gain the point,
but Dorothy's humour's out of joint.
"*I'd like to punch you on the chin.*"
'One more to go, but you can't win.

Twenty across, six letters no more.'
"*And the clue?*" she snarled, in a tigerish roar.
I shrugged my shoulders: 'It's nought,' I said ...
'... Though it might be an 'O' instead ...'

"*Oxygen!*' She yelled in triumph,
while I retreated, using some tact.
"*A draw. A draw. And still unbeaten.*"

She's not only smart:

But boy, can she act.

Polyopathy

is yapply hoot
and that should put the game afoot,
Life's not the same as once it was;
becoz, becoz, becoz, becoz.
Army style's no longer tops;
short back and sides at barbershops
and trousers at half-mast,
when styles would soon be changing fast.
The weather then was on parade;
Memories that never fade,
of seasons primed by bugle call.
Summer and Winter, the best of all.

But then the natives had the sense
to test Imperial pretence,
and Old Britannia, that Pantomime Dame,
fled from the stage, abandoning claim.
But what of the children still in the show?
Was it a case of quid pro quo?
Of course it was, but what came next?
An age that has the world perplexed.

So now, it's any style you choose,
Losers win, and winners lose.

Why did we sail o'er sea and foam?

To greet our sins returning home.

Every man mistakes the limits of his vision for the limits of the world. Schopenhauer

Polythemous

In a drunken stupor, he dreamt of food.
Crunching another captive's head.
Licking his lips for the last of the blood.
Swigging a drink, and then to bed.

Where now he sensed a dancing flame
advancing, advancing, slow but sure.
And heard a voice call out his name:
Confusing him more, because obscure.

He reached for his club, but touched the air.
His head began to throb and ache
as never before. He turned in despair,
intent on sleep. His second mistake.

Hands tightened ropes and made them fast.
The flame grew larger, then a pain
fired an explosion in his head
that seared connections to his brain.

Roaring in anger he broke his bonds
and ripped the stake from his bloody eye.
Cleared the way by swinging it round:
Happy to hear his enemy's cry

and the echoing sound of frightened feet.
Then silence. The rabbits had gone to ground.
He sensed they were among the sheep
but knew, tomorrow, they'd be found.

Thoughts lingered on, despite the pain:
They can't get out. They can't get out.
This cave is blocked by my treasured rock –
But in his dreams began to doubt ...

... No-man was sailing on the sea
with singing crew and billowed sails.
And he, on the island, stooping low;
following rams by holding their tails.

He cursed the Gods for their mocking mien.
His worth no more than a household slave:

Once a cave had been his home:

And now, No-man,
with stake and brand,

had made

his World

a cave.

Problem Child

I read in the paper the story of Kate,
who lived with her father, and sister.
Her temper was such; no one bothered her much,
and beau's, wanting wives, soon dismissed her.
Even psychologists, who should have known better,
never once made inquires, or called in to vet her.
Though psychology then, wasn't quite at the stage
to determine, what later became our heritage:
And secured a future for Sigmund Freud;
A situation he more than enjoyed.

But supposing his students could have explored
Kate's childhood memories, others ignored.
And found, perhaps the jealous streak,
that made poor Kate appear a freak.
Treating her with the talking cure
until she changed, and became demure:
Saying goodbye to strife.
Fulfilled, as a loving wife.

But Shakespeare had another ending.
For what is broken, still needs mending:
In life, as on the stage,
where actors need no therapy:
to put aside their rage:

But simply, turn the page.

Senses Matter

Suck a lemon, or swallow some tea.
Listen to nestlings up in a tree,
compete with each other, noisily:
Each one crying, ME, ME, ME.
See gathering clouds up in the sky.
Rainy day? Or sunny and dry?
Smelling mother's apple pie ...
Told to wait, you sit and sigh.
On the table, what a sight,
fresh out the oven, smells just right.
Taste buds bursting with delight;
till finally, you take a bite.
Silence descends on conversation.
Speaking is Eating's abomination.
Faces now shining with rare admiration
And then, our father's salutation:
"Your mother's the best in the world."

Touching, Tasting; Smelling, Hearing.
These are the senses that keep us cheering,
even when Oblivion's nearing;
when what we are, is disappearing.

Formed differently then, but still in Being:

Transformations, we won't be Seeing.

Sleepwalking

Imaginary gardens,
need no rain or sun.
Flowers there, stay open
long after day is done.
Such perfection once before
saw Mother Nature at her peak.
But that, in Eden long ago;
was more concerned with man's physique.

Since then, our brains, enlarged a bit,
have proved to be the perfect guide;
and scientists, more cautious now,
are focused on neurons linked inside.
A 'mental workspace' as it's been termed,
that acts much like computers do;
though internally, not in cyberspace,
and ends in something entirely new.
What wasn't once has come to be;
not as much by thinking.
But other-directed ways and means
of which we have small inkling.

Offspring of childlike revelries,

in gardens where stars are twinkling.

ADDRESS TO MOURNERS

We very rarely speak of the dead.
But I'm certain Jean would want this read
to celebrate her life, instead
of burying ourselves in sorrow.

Besides, she said to me one day
she talked to Len in the same way,
and he'd been gone for a long time:

So I'll do the same, if I may.

Speaking To Jean

I'll talk to you without a phone,
as I've done so many times before:
to try and keep you up-to-date
with all the things that you adore.

We'll talk about the cakes you've made,
each one delightful to the tongue.
The Christmases we've spent with you
and Len and Lisa: having fun.
The books you've read, the films you've seen,
The clothes you've bought for next to nowt.
The steaks, the pies, the sales, the shops:
the drinks you've drank, when you've been out.

What's that you say? My voice is fading?
The battery can't be going flat.
Maybe the volume just needs raising ...
... there, that's better.
It's great to chat.

Well, I better be getting ready.
Funerals never were my style:
But just for you, my lovely sister,
I'll put myself behind: this time.

Sackcloth and ashes have never appealed.
It's not my way, to display too much.
And a sorrowful mask is not for me:

But Jean, I'll be keeping in touch.

Special Favours

Of history's villains,
only one now survives:
But it's not just the Jews
who keep Hitler alive.

Neo-Nazis in Europe:
Extremists elsewhere.
All worship *Der Fuehrer*
as if he were there,
to honour their cause
with his Presence and Will.
Active, alive
and entrancing them still.

Historians too,
with new Russian docs
are questioning classics
with tackle and blocks.
Exposing new facts
to embellish their name.
Appearing on TV
to public acclaim.

But what makes a man
who is millions strong?

Believing in Right:

But doing, what's wrong.

Strong Men Feed On Iron

I've got a mate. I've got a chum,
who seems to think I'm Tweedledum.

Each time he gets a poem from me,
he always replies like Tweedledee.

When what I want is information,
not some childish aberration.

Some opinion, good or bad
bitter-tasting, or sugar-clad

and too extreme to give some hope;
enough to make a Shakespeare mope.

I'd bear it gladly with a cheer,
and even drink his health with beer.

Feasting myself on meagre fare,
if only there was something there.

But what can I do, when he replies
to each of my poems:

"Contrariwise?"

Suffering Art

Putting the pieces together,
the picture's nearly complete.
I nearly gave up in frustration:
Nearly admitted defeat.
For who, but the Lord has the power
to raise from death, the dead?
And the lad I'd loved for his laughter
was souring the Present instead.
Why? And how could I help him?
Fill him with *joie de vivre*?
Wishing that I were a wizard
with magical spells to weave.
Or Painter, Musician or Poet;
to speak in mysterious ways.
Healing with colours, word and song;
Ending the heart's malaise.
Yet discontent is not a sin,
Re: Vincent and his rages;
Pulling a razor on Paul Gauguin.
Boosting the Devil's wages.
It might be seen as evilness,
a vile abomination.
But equally, could be the germ
of a sublime creation.

And that's the dilemma
all artists embrace.
Except for the fool;

with a smile on his face.

Suffer The Little Children . . .

There once was a man
who would do any dare,
when still in his youth.
But now, with grey hair,
is happy to sit
in a comfortable chair;
breathing in lots
of Canadian air.

And when little children
(told to be fair)
have gathered, like pupils
around that old chair.
He regales them with tales
all picked up elsewhere.

But Canadian children
may sit there, and stare.
Though their dealings with adults
aren't quite on the square.
Pretending to parents
that they're unaware:
While knowing all adults
are full of

HOT AIR.

Sunset Street

I used to live in Sunset Street
where children had no cares,
and parents guided little lives:
Their darling teddy bears.

It was off to bed at six o' clock,
when we were very small.
Without a protest on our lips:
That wouldn't do at all.

And growing up, we played our games
together on the street.
Swinging round the lampposts:
Running on rubber feet.

Of motorcars we had no fear
for they were very, very dear.
And only seldom came our way:
Hooting a horn to spoil our play.

We told PC Plummer, who shook his head.
"Take down their number. It's water and bread
and jail for them, as we'll all see
such bad 'uns never get sympathy

from His Honour, the Judge: The best in town.
He's widely known for sending them down.
Now back to your games, my duty's done.
And yours, is to spend it in laughter and fun."

. . .

Now I've returned to Sunset Street
but have no stylish hair.
Nor teeth to flash as bait to catch
the girls who used to stare.

But churn inside, when youngsters pass
at lunch-time break en-masse.
With noisy laughter and shining hope:
Though Life's a slippery slope.

The world turns round, I'm witness to that
But sometimes I wonder, if I'm losing my hat.
Not understanding the words they speak:
It could be Norwegian. More probably, Greek.

But still the losers are smoking their 'cigs'
Blaming their luck and cursing the 'pigs'.

Such lives as these, come quick to end:

When all are foes; and none, a friend.

Takeover

Men talk less than women,
as husbands will concur.
Something that's always puzzled me;
although I too, defer.
Yet my mind is scientific
full of facts and figures,
with procedures quite specific –
at which my daughter sniggers.
Evolution's always first:
What advantage would it give?
Or equally, a mutant gene,
might well be an alternative.

And obviously, a mother's voice
stimulating a baby's mind,
can lay the one foundation stone
necessary to human kind.
A natural route to feminine power,
as Jesuits learned so long ago.
Though now, without indoctrination,
it's just a case of saying, no.
Gaining control by opting out;
leaving their babies squawking,
while busy in Brussels, for years on end:
contented, as long as they're

talking.

Terminus

after A. D. HOPE

The patient isn't patient.
He longs to find a bed.
The bed is waiting all alone.
There's only her, and Dread.

She has no one to comfort,
to warm her through the night.
To strip her in the morning,
and clothe in virgin white.

She too, becomes impatient.
But soon is on the mend,
When patient's heart stops beating:

All waiting's at an end.

The Best-Of-All Tools

Using a saw to cut some string,
is not a very sensible thing.
You'll snag the blade in tooth or notch,
when a sharpened knife would have saved a botch.

Using force to gain affection
is yet another misdirection,
bordering on sinning;
and stands no chance of winning.

At least, she'll never see you again.
At most, her brothers repay you with pain,
And then the judge, her cousin, will scowl,
when sentencing you for wickedness foul.

So heed the wisdom of the Wise:
Use artifice to gain your prize.
For Love dwells there, where Romance rules:
And soft, the words, unknown to fools,
that you should choose,

as the best-of-all

tools.

The Facts Of Life

Some say a mirror cannot lie.
Of course it can, I'll tell you why.

Remember the story of Snow White?
Her stepmother's mirror, being polite,
when asked, who's fairest of them all?
Said, "You are, of course. Don't you recall?
Is this some silly sort of game?
I told you yesterday, the same,
and I'll repeat, to prove it's true
It's you, it's you, it's YOU, IT'S YOU!"

"You can't mean me," Snow White replied.
"My stepmother says that I'm cross-eyed,
and lack the sense of a wombat worm.
Less like a lady, and more like a germ."

"Don't matter. What I say is true.
As true as cock-a–doodle-doo.
You'll be the bride of a handsome king
And all through life, you'll smile and sing.

Come, come, my child. Don't cry. Don't cry..."

But cry she did.

It was all a lie.

The Man Who Swallowed The World

'Let's have a holiday,' she said.
But why should I want to stray,
having a world inside my head
that's not so far away?
The trouble with Emily, you see,
isn't that she's from Venus.
It's just ... she's not the same as me:
A question of taste between us.

Nothing of major consequence,
we've lived our lives and got along;
have children, born with common sense,
who'd never agree to anything wrong.
But when the season comes around
and brochures litter the dining table,
I take my troubles underground:
As far as I am able.

While Emily, entranced, enchanted,
child-like, a magic carpet flies ...
Her every fantasy now granted
by photographs and floral lies.
Adieu, my love, I wish you well,
But not for me, this heathen Hell.
I'll stay at home, my flag unfurled:

Displaying a long forgotten world.

Them And Us

The people in authority
are just the same as you and me.
They may pretend to be above
corruption, dishonesty, unnatural love.

But then, we find to our surprise
they're thieves, adulterers, tellers of lies.
But feel a certain satisfaction
in our duplicitous reaction.

The pleasure that we hypocrites take
in punishing a fool's mistake:
Choosing some undeserving goat:
Leading it out,
and slitting its throat.

The truth is we are one with them:
The very people we condemn
as murderers, steeped in innocent blood,
are those confirming us as 'Good'.

To start again at the beginning:
if we are them, then both are sinning
and this, in turn, means no contemning:

Or else, it's us; we'll be condemning.

Then, And Now

When Pope sat down, and wrote on a page:
"… in soft bosoms dwells such mighty rage"
It gave me food for thought.

He's talking of women, if you hadn't guessed:
or more indiscreetly, about their breasts,
and emotions of a sort.

The sort, we usually attribute to men …
But to women? And way back then?
It gives one cause to think.

My history teachers weren't too clever.
Still, I know mores aren't forever
and generations link.

But surely the body is kept intact:
Women are women, and that's a fact.
Life produces life.

And men, of course, will be always needed
in person, or professionally seeded,
for spinster, lover or wife.

Women are loving, kind and caring.
Men are bold, and brave and daring -
that's how it used to be.

But stereotypes no longer apply
and even a stranger's an ok guy:
A regular bonhomie

who, under the surface, is seething with rage
being shortly compelled to return to his cage:
But then, invited, is willing

to walk her home, and sip her tea.
Enjoy the contact, pay the fee
and bid goodbye:

after killing.

Tyger, Tiger

Tyger, Tiger, it's a shame
captivity's not made you tame.
So many years inside a cage,
and all you do is rant and rage.

Yet on the pages of a book
you have a certain, noble look.
Not the killer that savages man,
but lord and leader of all your clan.
Aristocratic, always at ease,
eager for battle, slow to appease.
Adored by females and cubs you've sired;
Avoided by rivals, who quickly retired.
And free to wander where you will,
since no-one's there to wish you ill.

Except a grunting, screeching ape
waiting to make his BIG ESCAPE.
And then, you'll come within his reach:
A captive in the cage of speech.
Only a shadow of what you were;
lisping a soft and feline purr.

Tyger, Tiger, it's a shame
your second life has made you tame.
Though phantom females fill your cage:

Their very presence, confirms old age.

Uncertainties

"I am who I am, but who am I?"
It's a question asked many times before.
But surely one we can't ignore
by bolting the door, and saying: "Goodbye."

Existentially, needing to know;
This is the kind of mind we've got.
But still uncertain of Being, or Not:
And all too eager, with Yes, and No.

We're here, and then we take our leave:
Going nowhere though travelling far.
Way up to Heaven, to meet the Czar,
while down on Earth, our loved ones grieve.

At least, for some who share convictions
which they consider water-tight:
Commandments they can't overwrite
because of their need for restrictions.

Beliefs that all begin with: "Don't..."
Placing a gag on laughter,
while praising the life, hereafter:

And praying their progeny

won't.

Under Cover

Theirs is a dark and silent land;
a land that lies beneath the skin.
Always so close, so close at hand:
Always so hard to win.
Chained by our senses, thoughts and beliefs,
Habits inhibiting ventures bold.
Fears confirming, we'll come to grief.
Scars reminding us, Youth's now old.

There was a time, when Time stood still.
And anchored fast, we would not sail.
Having the strength, but not the Will
to chart a course, and then, to fail.
Not knowing then, that failure's best
to lure the lion from his cave
and put the whole man to the test;
to see if he's a knight, or knave.

But up above, or down below,
they're subject to the same regime:
For all is but a puppet show:

Where Puppet Masters reign supreme.

We All Have Our Moments

Two brothers, though you'd never guess:
One prim and proper, the other, a mess.
Both living side by side.
Pass each other in the side:
For conversation's obsolete,
unless it is applied.

The first is living with his wife.
The second live's where trouble's rife
and now, is there to stay.
They used to be the best of friends
until the Fates chose different ends
for them, one fading day.

Bored with management, lacking spice,
they entertained themselves with dice,
but quickly tired of that.
"What if we bet on human endeavour,
in moulding Fate?"
"Are **they** that clever?"
Everyone laughed:
"Fiat."

Two terraced houses both the same,
acted as starters in this sky-born game.
Two gardens fruit-full, ablaze with flowers
enchanted both brothers for hours and hours.

But one had Will, the other none:
And soon, two gardens reduced to one.
The second left to seed.
Jealousy took root in soil
abandoned now, for weeds to spoil
with ever growing speed.

Brambles and ivy snaked and sped,
improper thoughts flourished and spread
in such furtile ground.
Wickedness usurped his mind
and deeds were done, excessive, unkind:
But only to confound.

For suddenly, salvation neared:
And in the darkness, light appeared.

The Fates returned to common sense.

And that's made all the difference.

⸺◦❧◦⸺

What Did I Say?

Three pensioners meeting once in the year,
Once in the year when May is Queen;
Their Spring-time gone, but do they care?
Life's laws are there to contravene.
For men they are, and men they'll be,
Despite the fact, I disagree:
But find myself outvoted.
"We're over seventy years of age,
Why tempt the Fates living above?
They get no fees to help assuage
impish desires, to give a shove
when one or both look over the edge,
of a sharp and slippery granite ledge:
To find themselves promoted."
"Rubbish," they say, "It's so much bunk.
You're such a miserable fellow.
Maybe because you haven't the spunk,
Maybe you're coloured yellow."
I didn't argue. What's the use?
But notice laces working loose
And egos exceedingly bloated.
"Off you go then, pay no heed.
Take a chance, you might succeed.
But if you don't, and you should die …
I'll sing your praises,

bye and bye."

Who's Who?

Are people, people no matter what?
(Including religion, colour and class,
   sickness of body, spirit or mind.)
Or, in asking, am I being unkind?

In Russia, it used to be Comrades all,
but 'Animal Farm' put paid to that;
   until Reality followed suit
   now Capitalism's taking root.

Without our clothes, we're all the same;
   though not in shape, or sizes.
And those remaining covered up
   are probably the wisest.

People speak different languages.
   People have curious thoughts,
   Yet all in all, I'd guarantee
they're just the same as you and me.

But what if they're Aliens in disguise,
   with Laser Pistols up their sleeves,
while smiling smiles and speaking lies:

O Sons of Adam, Daughters of Eve?

Witness

To slake my curiosity
I asked the chap in the bed next to me,
"How does it feel to be dead?"
It took a while to make the link,
But then his eyes began to blink
as he pondered what I'd said.

"To tell the truth, I'm at the station
and haven't reached my destination.
I'm halfway in-between.
Officials here are very fussy:
Even the mice are drilled by a pussy,
wailing a doleful keen.

This is the first of seven stages.
It used to be three, but that was ages
ago. When? I don't know."
"1960. Cochran, his name.
We bunked off school. I took the blame.
But what a stupendous show."

A shadow fell upon his face.
"Missed it all. Bet it was ace:
Almost Heaven in fact . . ."
"Cheer up" I said "You've had your fun."
"Okay, Okay, but now it's done.
And never will be back."

"You can't say that. Reincarnation ..."
"Is unconfirmed, and no salvation:
To come back as a slimy toad
would take some adjusting;
and is more than disgusting:
It's a life that could only corrode."

"But isn't that what life's about?
After champagne, comes the sauerkraut.
Something we can't evade.

And if the Potter starts to sneeze,
And makes a piece that doesn't please:

It's still, at least, been made.

Wordsmith

Thoughts are words
not meant for herds,
but for oneself alone.
It's Nature's way
of keeping in play
notions you may disown.
For words themselves
persist like elves
in being mischief makers.
A spiteful wife
recalls to life
all you said at the baker's
years ago.
Then let's you know
it hurts her still today.
She loves you, now
but must allow
those memories to linger.
For if they wane
she couldn't complain:
Nor wrap you round her finger.
It's just as well
because farewell
would mean a great upheaval.

And I'm a guy
to whom good-bye
would be the rankest evil.
You might have guessed
another nest
is where I always head for.
And find at home
what others comb
the Pacific and the Med. for.
My pleasure's found
and triple-crowned
by bonnie Susie Leigh.
Who's on her own,
and always prone,
when hubby's off to sea.

A jolly tar
may travel far
and visit foreign wimmin'.
While I'm content
to waive the rent,

and debate the joys of sinnin'.

Why Ears?

How come we have ears, when others have none?
Were they gifts from a God? Who woke and said: "Bon!
They can listen to sermons, and then sing a song
    without bothering me in the morning."
Since he thought of this ploy, he can really enjoy
    the life that he's leading in heaven.
Whereas once he spent years, in answering prayers,
    now it's over by quarter past seven.

So God was pleased, but Darwin felt guilt,
when publishing papers long study had built.
Convinced that his theories would bring retribution
He dillied and dallied, and delayed Evolution.
Now everyone knows ears came from a jaw,
    redundant then, and furthermore,
moulded to bones which responded to sound:
Pleasing the Beatles, who became world renowned.

But this is how **we** understand it;
how **I** understood it, before she landed.
An Alien in a saucer, who said:
"Come here!" and I did as commanded.
"Kneel down" and I fell on my knees.
"Now that's why you mammals have hearing:

So **we** can control you, whenever we please."

Short Poems

Only Human

Mirror, mirror can't you see,
that you are just the same as me?
You're not a Saint, and I'm no buyer,
having found another liar.
I used to think you showed me Truth,
before I left precocious Youth
and settled on a broader path
of moderation, and belly-laugh.

So pardon me for my defection,
but it's the fruit of long reflection.

∽∂∾

Sly Buggers

Mirrors pretend
to be a friend
by showing friendly faces.

But when alone,
they always moan:

Wiping away the traces.

Sly buggers.

Attitudes

Youth may think: 'I'm here to stay.'
But mark the man who's old and gray;
and long a friend of Grief and Sorrow ...

Is he content,

to leave ...

tomorrow?

∾∽∾

Fame At Last

Not being a man
who's travelled far.
Instead of a coffin,
I chose a jar.

But bought this plot,
as if at home,
so you could stand
and read my poem.

Caution

I see the sense of what you're saying.
It's rational, and jigsaws well.
But words have a worth, revealed on weighing:

Unlike the man with goods to sell.

∽∾

Don't You Dare?

It's not the coward's heart who dares
to climb such old and rickety stairs
that barely bear the weight of age:

To end in triumph on the stage.

Carpe Diem

One seat
Is not a set.
One brick
is not a wall.
One thought
you won't forget:

One Life's

enough for all.

෴

Keeping Count

Of all my friends, I like him best
who comes to me with jape and jest.
Chameleon-like, unique and strange,
with mood and manner apt to change.
From morning smile to midnight scowl,
from feathered song to savage howl.
And when he comes I shout, hooray:

So welcoming . . .

another day.

Lightning Source UK Ltd.
Milton Keynes UK
UKOW02f0111240316

270783UK00001B/32/P